50 Ways to Excel in Your First Job (and in Life)

Because The Most Important Lessons For Young
Professionals Are The Things That No One Tells You

Antonio Neves

ISBN: 1530630134
ISBN 13: 9781530630134
Library of Congress Control Number: 2016904882
CreateSpace Independent Publishing Platform
North Charleston, South Carolina

Do something that brings you joy. You owe it to yourself.

Table of Contents

Introduction

TODAY, MY RÉSUMÉ reveals that I'm a nationally recognized speaker, an award-winning journalist, and an author. My experience includes working with top companies like NBC, Nickelodeon, PBS, BET Networks, Advertising Age, and Inc.com.

But when I first arrived in New York City to begin my career, my résumé was basically a blank page – except for the fact that I attended a state university not many people had heard of, and that I'd had a couple internships.

When I began my career, a Google search of my name (if Google existed then) would have provided almost no results. Of course, this was before social media platforms like Facebook, Twitter, LinkedIn, or Snapchat were ubiquitous.

So how did I go from an empty résumé to working with some of the top companies in the world? This book shares many of the steps I took to build a successful career and the intangible lessons I learned along the way – those simple yet critical nuggets of wisdom that will set you up for a bright future.

Many of these lessons I learned by making mistakes. Others I picked up from mentors. One thing is for certain: None of these lessons were taught to me as a college student and I didn't find them in any books.

I believe that regardless of the college that you attended, your major, or even your grade point average, you can have an exceptional career. What this requires shouldn't surprise you: Lots of hard work and some resilience, patience, faith, and a good sense of humor.

Life is about choices – the choices we do and do not make. Thank you for *choosing* to read this book. I expect great things from you and would love to hear about them.

Antonio Neves
an@theantonioneves.com
www.TheAntonioNeves.com
@TheAntonioNeves

1
Make A Decision

EVERY DAY, YOU have the opportunity to make a decision.

A choice to be exceptional, or a choice to be average.

You can't be both.

The exceptional are willing to do what others won't to succeed. The average follows the crowd and accepts "good enough."

"Good enough" is not enough.

2

If You're On Time, You're Late

ALWAYS SHOW UP early and plan ahead.

"Traffic was bad" is not an acceptable excuse.

If you're on time, you're late.

3

Find The Edge

"IF YOU'RE NOT close enough to the edge, then you're taking up too much space."

Finding the Edge means being willing to regularly get uncomfortable.

The only way a muscle can grow bigger is by lifting heavy weights. When you lift heavy weights, your muscle actually tears. Then something miraculous happens – it grows back bigger and stronger.

If you've ever been an athlete, you know that feeling you get before a game, match, or race begins when your heart starts racing and you get butterflies in your stomach? *That's Finding the Edge.*

If you've ever been a performer, you know that feeling you get before you take the stage when your palms get sweaty or your throat starts to feel dry? *That's Finding the Edge.*

And if you've ever had a crush on someone, you know that moment when you finally ask them out on a date and you stutter your words while you feel like your heart is going to explode? *That's Finding the Edge.*

Think about the last week of your life. Now think about the last month. When was the last time you felt that increased heart rate? When is the last time you felt that nervous energy? When is the last time you felt butterflies in your stomach?

When was the last time you found the edge?

If you don't find the edge and regularly get uncomfortable, odds are you aren't growing, developing, and moving forward in life.

Push yourself. Find the Edge.

4

Be An Opportunity Identifier

COMPLAINING AND BLAMING others because you're stuck is easy.

Top performers don't do this.

Instead, those who succeed acknowledge what's going on around them and figure out how to make their situation better.

Truly successful people take full responsibility and accountability for their actions. They do what they say they're going to do. They keep agreements.

Most importantly, they ask themselves what they can *learn* from each situation.

Be an opportunity identifier.

Instead of focusing on what's wrong, identify what's right and make it better.

5
Identify What's Most Important

AS A PROFESSIONAL, you're going to juggle a lot of responsibilities.

To make sure you stay on top of everything, it's critical to have a to-do list that identifies your biggest priorities.

Regularly ask yourself what's most important about today, this week, this month, etc. If you're unsure, ask your manager.

When you know what's important, it allows you to focus and deliver exceptional work.

6
Confidence Is Earned

IF YOU WERE miraculously dropped off at the top of Mount Kilimanjaro (at an altitude of over 19,000 feet), what would happen?

If you aren't an experienced mountaineer, you'd probably take in the view for a second and then pass out. You could even die from altitude sickness.

Why? Because your lungs haven't *earned* being at that high altitude.

This is the reason the careers of so many reality stars tend to run out of air so quickly. Two or three years after they win the big competition on television, they typically fade away.

Why? It's not necessarily that they aren't talented or gifted. It's because they haven't done the work necessary to get to, and stay, at the top of the mountain.

Before a comedian lands that big television special, she's worked for years practicing her craft and performing at small comedy clubs. Before the band you love sells out a stadium, they've played at countless small venues getting their sound just right.

Confidence is earned.

Be willing to do the work and earn your way to the top of the mountain. This way, instead of faltering or passing out, you can enjoy it and take in the amazing view.

7

You Have Two Ears
And One Mouth

THE MOST VALUABLE thing you can give someone is your attention.

Listen more than you talk.

Good listeners don't think about what they're going to say next when the other person is speaking.

Good listeners ask follow-up questions.

Good listeners make it all about the person they're with – not about them.

So put down your phone.

Listen.

Ask questions.

Say, "Tell me more about that."

Be genuinely interested in someone's story.

When you do this, you earn trust and can truly connect with others.

Listen more than you talk. This is how you become the most interesting person in the room.

8

Talk To Yourself More Than You Listen To Youself

THE MIND IS a powerful thing. Use it to your advantage.

What we focus our attention on with our thoughts – those worst-case scenarios that are often figments of our imagination – sometimes end up coming true because of the energy we put into them.

Instead of listening to your fears and thinking about all those things you don't want to happen, try talking to yourself.

Tell yourself what you *would* like to happen. Visualize it happening. Write it down.

Talk to yourself more than you listen to yourself.

9
Find People Who Make You Better

YOU CAN SPEND time with *Thieves* or *Allies*.

Thieves are those people who **never** encourage, support, or empower you. They don't challenge you. They don't inspire you. They don't hold you accountable. And they don't push you to be the absolute best version of yourself.

Thieves are energy vampires that zap all of your drive. *Thieves* always have drama going on. *Thieves* **settle for mediocrity.** *Thieves* **can bring out the worst in you.**

Allies are those people who **always** encourage, support, and empower you. They do challenge you. They do inspire you. They do hold you accountable. And they do push you to be the absolute best version of yourself.

Allies give you energy. *Allies* always have great things going on in their lives. *Allies* won't accept anything but the best. *Allies* bring out the best in you.

Think about the five people you spend the most time with and ask yourself this question: **Do they make you better?**

Identify the *Thieves* in your life and create boundaries.

Find your *Allies* and keep them close. Be an ally to others.

Don't be afraid to work with the best. Surround yourself with greatness.

10
Release What You Can't Control

IN LIFE, THERE are things you can control and things that you can't control.

You can't control the weather, but you can use an umbrella to stay dry in the rain.

Focus on what you can control in any given situation.

Release what you can't – worrying will get you nowhere.

11

Be The CEO Of Your Career

REGARDLESS OF YOUR title, remember that you are the CEO of your own career.

An employee waits for instructions and does work that's "good enough."

But having a CEO mindset means that regardless of your title, you:

Proactively seek out opportunities and "special assignments" to contribute.

Set actionable goals for yourself.

Build relationships across the company, not just in your department.

Stay on top of industry news, trends, and the latest research.

Read books.

Deliver *more* than expected.

Conduct informational meetings (See #23).

Take continuing education courses.

Articulate what you want.

Understand your brand and career goals.

When you have a CEO attitude, you aren't just going to work – you're building a future.

12
Your First Job Won't Be Your Last

YOUNG PROFESSIONALS REGULARLY worry about making the wrong choice when it comes to their first job.

Good news: There's no right or wrong decision. Why? Because your first job won't be your last job.

The job market and economy has changed. People no longer have lifelong employment. Actually, people now change jobs every two years on average.

So there's no need to stress yourself out wondering if you're selecting the "right job." Instead, get curious.

Ask yourself if there are great development opportunities in whatever job you select.

Ask yourself if the job is in a city that you're excited to explore.

Ask yourself if you'll be challenged.

Turn whatever fear you're feeling into excitement and always remember: There is no wrong decision.

Your first job won't be your last job.

13
Find Good Friction

FRICTION CAN BE a good thing.

Imagine that you're lost in the woods and cold, but you have two sticks and some kindling. When you rub those sticks together, you create *friction* that can start a fire.

Now, imagine that you're in a car and it's stuck in the snow with the tires spinning. The car won't move. If you put some sand or salt underneath the tire, you can create some *friction* to help the car move forward.

Consider this: Diamonds are formed from carbon under millions and millions of years of pressure. Their beauty comes from friction.

In your career, seek out *good friction*.

Get feedback on your projects from colleagues. Spend time with allies because they're going to hold you accountable and not accept your excuses. Be willing to share your opinion even if it goes against what everyone else believes.

Good friction is where growth, development, and breakthroughs happen.

14

Ideas Are Useless…

…UNLESS YOU BREATHE life into them.

Don't show up to a meeting with *just* an idea.

Prior to sharing an idea with your manager or team, do as much research as possible, find successful examples in the marketplace, be prepared to answer any challenges, build a prototype, etc.

Make it easy for people to say yes to your project or idea.

15

Your Personal Brand Is...

...WHAT PEOPLE SAY about you when you're not around.

Open up a private web browser and Google your name.

What do the search results show? Is it actually you? Is it someone who has the same name as you? Is it something that you posted on social media that you're embarrassed about?

The good news is that you can influence search results by building a strong personal brand.

First, use a free web service like about.me to create a free personal website (i.e., about.me/antonioneves). Once you build it, use this link in your email signature and social media profiles.

Second, create a LinkedIn profile. You'll find that LinkedIn will serve you more as you gain more experience in your career.

Next, go to a website like register.com and buy your name (i.e., www.yourname.com). It should cost you less than $15.

Control what comes up when someone Googles you so you can be proud of what people find.

16

Communicate Like A Pro

BEING ABLE TO communicate with confidence is a game-changer.

It's the difference between getting people to believe in you or forget about you.

If an employer trusts you, they'll hire you for that dream job.

If your manager is inspired by your passion, they'll invest in you and your development.

If fellow colleagues believe in you, they'll get behind your new idea.

Many people struggle with communication skills and feel painfully awkward. If this is you, don't stress.

The best way to become a better communicator is to study great communicators, regularly take communication courses, and practice, practice, practice.

17

It's Not Who You Know...

...IT'S WHO KNOWS *you*.

You may be familiar with a lot of people, but if they're not familiar with you, your work, and your goals, who you know will do you no good.

Reintroduce yourself to people. Remind them of who you are and what you're looking to accomplish in your career. Act as your own public relations department.

Build strong relationships on and offline that create value for others.

18
Dress For The Job
That You Want

"BUT EVERYONE WEARS jeans..."

Regardless of your title or position at a company, pay close attention to those who hold the job that you would like to have one day.

How do they dress? How do they present themselves? Take note, learn, and emulate.

Dress for the job that you want, not the job that you have.

19
Know Your Story

OVER THE COURSE of your career, you're going
to regularly get asked, "What's your story?" or "Tell
me about yourself."

Don't let this question catch you off guard.

Most people give a chronological response to questions like these.

*"Well...I was raised in X town...I went to X college...I
studied X... I work for X...I live in X..."*

These answers, while not wrong, are boring. Instead,
get creative with your answer.

Take time to identify a few things about you, your
story, your background, and journey that make you
unique. These are those things that would never show
up in a Google search or on your résumé.

20

Say It Before You Run Out Of Breath

"SO WHAT DO you do?"

You'll regularly get this question in elevators, at networking events, and at parties.

Always have an answer ready to go – but with one rule: By the time you run out of breath, you should have completed your answer.

The easiest way to answer this question is by including the *position, industry,* and *type of company* you work with (or are looking to work with).

For example: *"I work as a junior account executive with the advertising agency XXX."*

When you're clear and concise, your reward will be hearing that coveted, "Tell me more about that."

21
Take Accountability
And Responsibility

WHEN SOMETHING GOES wrong and you're responsible for it, don't make excuses, ignore it, or blame someone else.

Instead, take full accountability and responsibility for the role that you played, and learn from it.

This is what integrity and strong character is all about.

22
Stay Open

ALWAYS STAY CURIOUS.

When you receive feedback and suggestions, even if it's tough to hear, process it from an open point of view rather than a defensive one.

Even when you disagree, regularly ask, *"What can I learn from this?"*

Sometimes feedback or red ink on a big project can be a major learning opportunity for you to grow and develop.

23
The Most Powerful Meeting You Can Have

THE MOST POWERFUL meeting that you can have isn't a job interview. It's an informational meeting.

An informational meeting is an opportunity to meet with someone you can learn from. It's a great way to expand your network, increase your influence, and build your brand.

The best way to secure an informational meeting is to tap into your existing network. Your network includes your colleagues, family and friends, friends of friends, former professors, college alumni networks, social networks, people you've met at networking events, and beyond.

Once you identify people to contact, send them a brief email. Introduce yourself, share how you came across them, and tell them a little about yourself. From there, ask for 15 minutes of their time for an informational meeting to discuss what you would like to learn from them.

Once you secure the meeting, *prepare* as much as possible. Learn as much about the person, their background, and their work as you can. Review any information about them on the Internet. Prepare great questions and have a goal of what you'd like to get out of the meeting.

During the meeting, the focus should be on them. You're there to learn and to be a sponge. Soak up their wisdom. Most of the time, the meeting will shift to you. When it does, be ready to talk about your aspirations and goals and to share your story.

Let's be clear – an informational meeting is not a job interview.

Asking for a job or providing an unsolicited résumé during an informational meeting is the fastest way to lose trust. Instead, be so impressive that they want to learn more about you.

End the meeting by asking, *"Is there anyone else you think I should meet?"* If they're impressed by your preparation and questions, they'll gladly refer you to someone for another informational meeting.

Lastly, follow-up by sending a handwritten thank you card **(see #44).**

24

Before You Hit 'Send'…

… ALWAYS REREAD WHAT you wrote.

Writing is serious business. People notice good, clear writers.

Whether it's an email, letter, or article, sending out your first draft without giving it a second look isn't good enough.

Ask yourself, *"Does this make sense? Is what I'm asking for clear and concise? Is there information I shouldn't include?"* Because once it's out there, there's no hitting 'delete.'

Reread it for mistakes.

Tighten it up.

Cut it in half.

Keep only the essential.

25
Don't Tell The Whole Story

ATTENTION SPANS ARE getting shorter and shorter. This is an unfortunate reality.

Keep this in mind the next time you share a story with your manager, team, or colleague.

Your opportunity is to share those things that are essential – the things that make people lean in and want to learn more.

Have a beginning, middle, and end. Know where you're going with the story.

Tell a story, not the whole story.

26
Winging It Is Easy When You're Well Prepared

IF YOU'RE ONLY prepared to "wing it," then be prepared to fail.

Instead, prepare like your career depends on it.

Do your research like there's going to be a test.

Put the time in to build your confidence.

Do the work that others won't.

Repetition is your friend.

It's easy to go off script when you know the script in the first place.

27

Be A Regular

HAVE A GO-TO spot.

A go-to café. A go-to restaurant. A go-to yoga studio. You get the idea.

When you do this, over time you'll build strong relationships with people outside of your usual circle. You'll get to know the staff, and even the other regulars, and they'll get to know you. Treat them well and they'll treat you even better.

Have a place where everybody knows your name.

28
Create Your Own Momentum

IF YOU FEEL stuck, take action.

As the author Seth Godin says, don't wait for others to pick you. Instead, pick yourself.

Make a decision. Pick up the phone. Complete an old project. Start a new project. Schedule an informational meeting.

By taking action, we create our own momentum.

29

When You Don't Know What To Do…

TALK TO A colleague or mentor that you trust.

Pick up the phone and call a friend.

Go for a walk in nature.

Say a prayer.

Write in a journal.

Work out at the gym.

Read an inspiring book.

When you don't know what to do, do something.

30
Be Better Together

DON'T DO IT all by yourself.

Together = Better.

Bring out the best in others and allow them to bring out the best in you.

31

Four Questions To Ask When Things Go Bad (*Or Good)

WHAT HAPPENED?

Why did it happen?

What role did I play in it?

What can I/we do to ensure this *never* happens again?

*What can I/we do to ensure this *does* happen again?

32
Ask "By When?"

GET CLARITY ON when something will be completed or should be delivered.

Answers like *"I'm working on it"* or *"We'll have it soon,"* aren't acceptable.

Get a firm date and time and hold people accountable.

33
How To Get Vacation Time

DON'T ASK. TELL.

Most people request vacation time or a day off like this: *"Can I have Tuesday off?"* or, *"I'm writing to request the week of the 15th off for vacation."*

This approach makes it easy for a manager to reject your request.

Instead, *tell* your manager what you're going to do. For example, *"I'm going to take Tuesday off,"* or, *"I'm taking the week of the 15th off for vacation."*

When you tell instead of ask, the decision has already been made.

34
Set Others Up For Success

WHEN YOU HELP others shine, you shine.

Be an ally to someone.

Set others up for success.

35
Confirm Communication Has Been Received

MAKE NO ASSUMPTIONS.

When someone communicates with you or asks you something (face-to-face, on the phone, or online), confirm that communication has been received.

If you're having a conversation with someone, paraphrase back to them what they said (*i.e. If I hear you correctly, you would like X delivered on Y date. Is that correct?*).

If you're communicating with an email, letter, instant message, or voicemail, don't assume the message went through.

If someone hasn't responded in an appropriate amount of time, follow up.

With this approach, you'll avoid a lot of miscommunication.

36
"We" Is Greater Than "Me"

BE INCLUSIVE.

Regularly audit your speaking and writing to see if you're making it solely about you or including others. Make sure you aren't inadvertently excluding people.

It's all about the "us" and the "we." This is what brings us together.

"I" and "me" keeps us apart.

37
Everyone Has A Job To Do

DON'T FEEL BADLY about asking someone to
do what he or she is supposed to do.

Seriously, don't.

However, do explore the emotions that you feel
around this to learn more about potential blocks or ten-
dencies that could impact your career long-term.

38
The Budget Isn't An Excuse

REGARDLESS OF THE budget, do your best to think big.

You can always rein in your idea to meet reality. But if you start with small thinking, you aren't leaving any room to surprise yourself with new possibilities.

Pro Tip: If you come in under budget on a project, they'll expect you to come in under budget every time. Use your resources.

39

"This Is How We've Always Done It..."

THIS STATEMENT IS never acceptable.

When there's room for improvement, improve.

Don't settle for mediocrity.

40
Have An Agenda

BE PROACTIVE, NOT reactive.

If you approach a job interview or performance review by only being prepared to answer the questions that you're asked, you're not setting yourself up for success.

Your job is to go into situations like this with an *agenda*.

Whether the meeting lasts 5 minutes, 30 minutes, or an hour, besides answering their questions, make sure you find creative ways to share key things that the employer or manager *must* know about you.

These include life and professional experiences that make you unique, or successes that don't always get measured with awards and accolades.

Find the things that people must know about you – those things that don't typically make it onto a résumé. Doing this will help you stand out from the crowd and distinguish yourself from the competition.

41
Just Because You're Good At Something…

…DOESN'T MEAN THAT you're supposed to be doing it.

Over the course of your career, you're going to find jobs that you excel at. Sometimes, the things you happen to be exceptionally good at are things that you really don't enjoy doing.

This poses a dilemma: *I'm good at this, but I don't like it.*

So what do you do?

Well, you can keep doing what you're good at and allow many months, and maybe years to pass you by. Or, you can pivot, and pursue those things that truly interest you.

If you're lucky, you'll find what Gay Hendricks in his book, *The Big Leap*, calls your "Zone of Genius"

Always remember: Just because you're good at something, doesn't mean that you're supposed to be doing it.

42

What Makes You Happy May Make Others Uncomfortable

YOUR FAMILY AND friends won't always understand.

And that's ok.

People who've known us for most of our lives view us in a certain way. When we make decisions that they disagree with, or when we take the road less traveled, this can knock them off balance.

Most of the time, our family and friends want what's best for us. But what's best for *them* isn't always what's best for us.

Have an honest talk with people. Share why you're making the decision that you're making. Listen to their concerns and then, make the decision that's right for *you*.

At the end of the day, the decision is yours.

43

You Can't Measure Grit

A PIECE OF paper doesn't tell the whole story.

When the New England Patriots defeated the Seattle Seahawks in the 2015 Super Bowl, there was something missing on the football field. Not a single starter in the Super Bowl was a "5-star athlete" coming out of high school.

5-star athletes are regarded as the best of the best. Yet, the most prestigious, high profile football game was being battled out by two star quarterbacks who weren't even close to being top draft picks.

This could be the case for you. Maybe you didn't attend a top ranked university or have the most in-demand skills. You may not look good "on paper."

However, always remember: A piece of paper doesn't tell the full story. It can't measure grit and resilience. It can't measure *potential*.

Algorithms searching for key words won't find commitment, dedication, and hard work.

Stay creative, offer new perspectives, work hard, and don't give up.

If you're the diamond in the rough, you won't be for long.

44

Write Handwritten Thank You Cards

NO, THESE AREN'T old-fashioned.

When someone does something kind for you, don't just send an email and be instantly delete-able. Instead, write a handwritten card and mail it to them.

This shows that you took the time to purchase stationery, write a note by hand, and venture to the post office to mail it.

Handwritten thank you cards allow you to be memorable. They go a long way.

The time it takes to write requires us to push pause on life to acknowledge someone else's kindness or generosity.

45
About Your Next Job

NEW JOB OPPORTUNITIES can be exciting.

They can come with new titles, new responsibilities, and a larger salary.

Here are two things to consider when you're considering a new job:

The work: Will you grow, learn, and be challenged?

Who you work for: Will they help you grow, learn, and be challenged?

46

Do The Work.
Forget The Title.

IF YOU EVER have to pick between a new job title and a raise, go with the raise.

Don't get caught up with titles. Instead, get caught up with doing exceptional work.

Great work gets recognized and rewarded.

47

When You Win An Award…

BRING YOUR WHOLE team on the stage with you.

Recognize the work others have done to support you.

48
Give Thanks. Give Back.

AT THE END of each day, find a way to give thanks and acknowledge all that's good in your life.

You can do this through prayer, writing in a gratitude journal, or meditating on all that's good.

Sure, everything may not be perfect. Maybe you had a rough day, week, or year. But there's always something to be grateful for. This includes shelter, food, clothing, friendships, and so much more.

It's important to remind ourselves of this every day.

Then, give back. This doesn't require money. All it requires is your time. There's always someone who could use some support and guidance.

Give back. Share what you've learned with others.

49

It's Just Water

ONCE WHEN I was in Juneau, Alaska, I noticed that something was off.

It was raining. But no one, *except me*, was using an umbrella. No one.

It didn't make any sense.

So, I walked up to a local to solve this mystery. The guy I approached was wearing glasses and they were covered with large droplets of water from the rain, as was his jacket, pants, and shoes.

"Sir, I'm from out of town," I said. "I noticed that none of the locals are using an umbrella. Why is this?"

After looking at me and my large umbrella he said, *"You know man, it's just water."*

I was floored. *It's just water!*

At once, everything made sense. Before I could say anything more, he walked away.

So when you're having a bad day on the job, things aren't going your way, or you get caught in a real rainstorm, remember that it's just water.

In time, it will always dry.

50
No One Cares...

...MORE THAN YOU,

No one cares more about your life, career, and goals than you do.

Yes, your parents care.

Yes, your friends care.

Yes, your significant other cares.

Yes, your manager cares.

Yes, your co-workers care.

But no one can, or should, care *more* than you.

Finally…

ENJOY THE JOURNEY.

The ups. The downs. The in betweens. All of it.

Because none of it matters unless you have fun.

Acknowledgements

THANK YOU TO all of the young professionals who regularly inspire me.

Thank you Pete Danielsen and Keith Brown for taking a chance on me when I was a young professional just beginning my career.

Thank you to Katie Hendricks and The Hendricks Institute for teaching me how to take a conscious approach to life.

Thank you to Shiwani Srivastava for editing this book

Finally, thank you to my wife and all of my mentors and allies who challenge me to be the best version of myself and provide "good friction."

About The Author

Antonio Neves is an internationally recognized speaker, writer, and author on leadership, communication, and the millennial workforce.

The go-to expert on helping young professionals achieve their potential, Antonio delivers keynotes and workshops to corporate and trade association audiences, recent college graduates and university students.

An award-winning journalist, Antonio worked in the television industry for 10 years as a correspondent, host, and producer with top networks including NBC, PBS, BET Networks, and Nickelodeon. Antonio's business articles regularly appear in Inc.com and Entrepreneur. com.

A former NCAA Division I student-athlete, Neves is the author of *50 Things Every College Student Should Know* and *Student Athlete 101: College Life Made Easy On & Off The Field.* A graduate of Western Michigan University and the Columbia University Graduate School of Journalism, Antonio lives in Los Angeles with his beautiful wife and two kids.

To Learn More, Visit:
www.TheAntonioNeves.com

Join the Conversation on Facebook, Twitter and YouTube:
@TheAntonioNeves

For Booking:
Tel: 888-559-7629
email: booking@theantonioneves.com

54138010R00049

Made in the USA
San Bernardino, CA
08 October 2017